Who Dares to Heal

by

Kathleen Ensko

Shivelight Press

Published in the USA and the UK

by Shivelight Press

an imprint of
MASTERWORKS INTERNATIONAL
27 Old Gloucester Street
London
WC1N 3XX
UK

Email: admin@mwipublishing.com
Web: http:/www.mwipublishing.com

Printed by Createspace
ISBN-13: 978-1497316843

copyright © Kathleen Ensko 2014

Cover by MWI Design

The statements, opinions and facts contained in this publication are solely those of the author Kathleen Ensko and not of the publisher and the editor(s).

All rights reserved. No part of this book or other material may be reproduced in any form without written permission of the publishers.

Who Dares to Tread

The events portrayed here are true although the names of people and places have been changed

24/4/2014

Thanks Brigid
From Kathleen

Chapter 1

I knew Una from the day she was born. She was the second daughter of the couple next door to me. Two boys came along later but I am writing about Una because she fascinated me. From an early age she had a will of her own and great sense of justice regarding people and animals. She was a happy, cheerful, loving child, who the neighbours in Sea View Place referred to as a tomboy. When she was still in her in her teens, she emigrated to England. Her family was sad to see her go, but all the young people had to emigrate at that time because there nothing for them in Ireland. She found work in a children's orphanage where she worked as a child care assistant for five years. She then left to work for a local authority, where she worked as a deputy for two years. She made a lot of friends in both places, some of whom she is still in touch with today. Una was a great believer in training. She felt it would give her a better insight into the needs of the children she would be looking after, so she applied for a place on a training course and was accepted.

Her many visits home to see her family were very happy times, and she would always be sad saying goodbye again. She often told me she wished her work was closer to home so that she could visit her parents more often. She worried about them in case they got ill. Una was seconded by the local authority where she worked before going on her training course. When Una finished the training course, she was placed in reception in a care centre. It was the hardest, but nevertheless, her greatest experience. On one of her visits home when she was telling me about it, she would laugh and say how shy she felt talking at case conferences and giving her views on different cases. She never tired telling me about a visiting psychiatrist who helped her overcome this, little did he realise what trouble and how harassed she would later be for being able to do just that when she later returned to Ireland. But then, she was advised never to go back to Ireland to work in any kind of a caring capacity because it would drive anyone with her experience mad, because they had their heads buried in the sand. At the time, Una did not believe it, but later found out for herself, I am sad to say.

When Una got married in 1974 to a quiet, refined man from Quash town in County Clare, the wedding took place in a little church in Sea View Place. Two years later, they returned to live in a country place called Rippling Rivers. I was delighted to have them back in our midst once more. Una commenced working for a local authority in September 1977. I am sure she remembers that day as if it were yesterday. Her organiser at the time was a very cheerful, outgoing type of person, by the name of Mary Hunt. Una liked her. Una was employed as a full time 'Help at Home' in Moss Town area. On her first day, she was told to go to the local Clinic and one of three nurses working there would introduce her to the patients or clients she was to visit until further notice. She referred to the people she visited as patients or clients because, depending on the needs of the person, the help at home was intended to be a 'go between' for the social workers in the board and the medical services. The nurse who took Una around on her first day was a kind, considerate, lady who had been doing community nursing when Una was a girl. Her name was Pat Stevens and she had years of experience and was aware of how isolated one could feel working in the community. Una told me that she would stop for a chat when they would meet on their rounds. On her second day, her organiser took Una to a man in a wheel chair. He was as a big man and needed a lot of attention because of his condition. Una's duties were general cleaning, making beds, washing and changing patients, giving patients their meals and medication, as well as to be aware of any deterioration in the patients' health so as to notify the patient's doctor or nurse. Also included were emptying commodes, collecting prescriptions, emptying and changing catheter bags when necessary, assisting nurses to give enemas and bed baths, shopping for clients, collecting and delivering laundry, collecting pensions and paying bills. She was also to assist deprived and needy families and numerous other tasks which would enable people to remain in their own homes.

Because of the different types of needs Una came into contact with, the training and experiences she had gained during the years of child care in London were beneficial to her, or so she thought. If she was to know then, what she was to discover later, I do not suppose she would have wanted to continue working for the 'Blue Bell Board' under any circumstances. How was she to know that no matter how hard she was to work as a 'Help at Home' or how capable or reliable she may be, it would only need a nurse to complain about her, either to the nursing supervisor or her organiser, that the nurse's word would be taken, regardless whether it be true or false.

On 6th December 1977 another Help at Home had commenced working in Moss Town. Her name was Frances Bruce and because she did not drive at the time, the patients and clients Una had been visiting were passed onto Frances. Una was allocated out of town to work in every direction. It entailed more travel, and because she was covering needy cases in all three areas of Moss Town, it was difficult for her to please the nurse in each area. Two of the nurses, who were in Moss Town when Una commenced work there, had now moved and they were replaced by two relief nurses, Barbara O'Connor and Lorna Flannery. These two seemed to want to show their authority over the 'Help at Home' staff, and although a lot of the patients did not require Una to wash their floors they were frightened of losing her because the relief nurse would have been and told them to get the 'Help at Home' to wash their floor etc. I often thought then, that if the nurses employed by Blue Bell Board did the job they were getting paid to do, and the 'Help at Home' was organised by the person that was getting paid to do that job, the Blue Bell Board might be in a much sounder financial state today. Because of the needs of the patients Una was visiting, she was much more involved with the nurses than Frances Bruce was. This continued when the two relief nurses were replaced by two permanent nurses with the Blue Bell Board.

Until Una went to work as a 'Help at Home' she regarded nurses as a responsible, reliable, professional group of people. I was amazed to discover how very unfairly and unprofessionally they treated her. Although she did experience how catty they could be to each other and about each other, it was amazing to her how they ganged up together and condoned wrong behaviour when dealing with someone outside their own profession. The organiser, Mary Hunt, resigned from the service and the Help at Home Service continued with an acting organiser by the name of Joan Collins. When the position was advertised Una applied for it. However, before she was due to go for interview, a relief nurse, Barbara O'Connor, who had previously reported Una for not doing what she asked her to do intervened. Needless to say, she did not explain that she had wanted Una to go and light a fire for a lady in her area at the same time as Una was assisting a nurse in another area with a bed bound patient. Una was not asked for any explanation about it - the nurse's word was automatically taken. Una did not have a chance of getting the position. Looking back on it later, Una said to me she thought it was a blessing in disguise that she did not get the position. As it happened, no one was appointed at that time and the service continued under the acting organiser.

Chapter 2

At this stage I would like to explain that I am not condemning all nurses. I am writing only about Una's personal experiences and I am sure that there are many nurses who would be ashamed to be associated with any Board which would allow an individual to be treated in this manner. But the persons in senior positions are the ones that have to take responsibility for making sure that this kind of thing does not happen. However, as time went by, things for Una were to become much worse and eventually they got to the stage where her own health was to suffer as a result.

Joan Collins, the first acting organiser, gave up the position. She was a kind, thoughtful person and I know Una was very sorry to see her go. In her place was Lorna Flannery, whom I referred to earlier when she was doing relief work in Moss Town. On February 14th, 1979, there were two more cases added to Una's workload. Because of where they were situated, Una was expected to travel twelve miles each morning without any travel allowance. She was allowed to claim for four and a half miles from Rippling Rivers, her own home town in the opposite direction to Moss Town, and the return. Una resented this very much as she believed that once one commenced work one should get the travel expenses one is entitled to. The Help at Home service was low in numbers and not many of them belonged to a trade union and so it took until the 1st of December, 1983 before this was rectified.

By this time a permanent Help at Home organiser was well established. The amount of training the Help at Home group was given over the years was very limited and there was very little ground covered that Una had not already done during her training and experience as a child care officer. Nevertheless, she enjoyed the courses and the sharing of experiences amongst the group. To Una the training courses were more like refresher courses but she explained to me that one never stops learning and so she enjoyed them and came away refreshed. She explained however, that her most valuable experience was field work. She gained a tremendous amount of experience from assisting the nurses in the areas. What the nurses did to her in the years that followed was more of a reflection on their ability to feel that they were capable of training somebody working with them, than on Una's ability to learn. I think this can be looked on as a big disappointment. Una was under the impression that one of the roles of a nurse working for the Board was to train families to care for their loved ones.

Over the years, many different nurses were employed in Moss Town and I am pleased to say that

Una does not have bad memories of all of them, as a matter of fact; some of them treated her on an equal basis. Nevertheless, when one gets treated badly by a few it makes one wonder whom one can trust. Frances Bruce, the other Help at Home worker in Moss Town and Una became good friends and were able to confide in each other. Frances had now got herself a car and was able to take on cases outside of the town. It was nice for both of them. When they would have a difficult case they could go together and bring their own cars on alternate days.

Una's problems started in earnest when, in January, 1983, a close relative suddenly got very ill and although neighbours tried to locate Una at work through the Post Office in Moss Town (the staff in Moss Town Post Office did try to get a message to Una through Pat Duggan, one of the nurses in the area, but Pat said she did not know where to locate Una) by the time Una arrived home it was too late to phone Ann Hughes, her organiser, to say that she would not be at work the next day. With no phone in the relatives home at that time, and due to the fact that Una was up most of the night caring for her relative, it was mid-morning before Una, who had to go a mile to the nearest phone, could let her organiser know that she was not at work. Una was vigorously reprimanded for not phoning earlier. Una tried to explain to Ann Hughes. When she asked if it would be possible for her to have unpaid leave in order to keep her relative at home, this request was refused and Una was told she had to take the remaining twelve days annual leave. Una was upset over this, as she had already made arrangements regarding her annual leave. Later that day, Una wrote to Ann Hughes putting her point. When her organiser received her letter she phoned Rockhill Post Office and insisted that the operator, an obliging lad by the name of Fred White, give a message to Una that she had to phone her boss immediately. The operator was disgusted by the tone of the message and informed Una that if anybody treated him in that manner he would retort in like manner. It was not surprising that there was a heated discussion on the phone and Una told Ann Hughes to get off her back. Ann Hughes in turn threatened what would happen to Una when she returned to work. Through her own efforts, Una eventually got one month's unpaid leave.

On the third day of resuming work, Una got a letter from her organiser asking her to meet her in the clinic at Moss Town. Una was never one to take things lying down and when she told me of the meeting I had a good idea that there would be an argument. What I did not know was that Ann Hughes would have the power to make Una incapable of continuing work that day and that she would have to get medical help as a result. It surprised me even more when Una told me that she saw two permanent nurses crouch past the window of the clinic in order that Una would not see them. Ann Hughes shouted even louder when she became aware of their presence in the clinic. At this stage the trade union got involved and arrangements were made for Una to see Dr Spillane who was an acting director of the Blue Bell Board and who treated Una very professionally. However, things did not improve for Una as Ann Hughes would take every opportunity to have a go at her.

Chapter 3

One of the nurses by the name of Joan Moran and Una became good friends. They would go together in the nurse's car to do heavy cases in her area, as well as the cases where it was advisable for two people to go together for moral support. Una could not work as closely as that with somebody without forming a close relationship. Una and Joan would discuss lots of things together, including experiences they both had during their training, both in different fields. I remember on one occasion Una telling me that nurses must have very limited training in family affairs. They appeared to be under the impression that child abuse and child sexual abuse could not possibly happen in Ireland. This would annoy Una as she felt that such things did happen but were swept under the carpet. Una was under the impression that because she treated such discussions as confidential that Joan did likewise. Unfortunately, Joan would tell the other nurses what Una had said, and in turn, it would be told to Una's organiser, twisted, and not as Una would have said it. Lots of things that Una was accused of by her organiser would puzzle her. For example, Una would commence work at 9.30 a.m. and do two or three calls before going to the clinic to meet Joan at 11 a.m. Una's organiser often accused her of commencing work at 11 a.m. which was totally untrue. It was on one of these visits to the clinic on 27th November 1985, that Pat Duggan, another nurse, informed Una that she had crashed her car in the snow the day before. She asked Una if she would go with her on the first call as she was feeling nervous going on her own. Una said she would go if Joan agreed to wait for her as she could not help both of them at the same time. They had a little moan between themselves but eventually agreed. Pat was complaining to Una on the journey and saying that Joan thought she owned Una. To make a long story short, when they returned Joan had gone to the patient they usually did together. Una had no choice but to follow her out to the patient's house as the patient's laundry was in Una's car. This entailed extra mileage. So, it was not surprising that Joan and Una had a few cross words before each going their own way. Una was not one to bear malice although she would stick up for herself if she knew she was right, no matter what position the accuser held. The next day however, when Una visited the clinic as usual, Pat Duggan was on annual leave and in her place was Barbara O'Connor. Joan was telling Barbara about what had happened and how Una had helped Pat instead of her. Una informed Joan that she had not discussed it with anyone and told Joan it was in bad taste for her to discuss it with someone else. Una emphasised very strongly the importance of helping each other without being catty about it. To make it worse for Una, Joan was discussing it with the nurse that had reported her years earlier, when a similar situation had occurred. As it happened, the relief nurse decided that there was no need for Una to help her as there was a part time 'Help at Home' already visiting that patient. After that, Una felt that when she visited the clinic there was an atmosphere there which was by no means pleasant.

Una thought it best to meet Joan at an arranged place instead of at the clinic and this was agreed to. On the 8th January 1986, Joan Moran was late meeting Una. It was a very cold frosty morning and very unpleasant sitting in a cold car. Una had her eyes fixed on the road expecting every minute to see Joan approaching. In the end, the cold got the better of her and she slipped into a nearby cafe for a cup of coffee. When eventually Joan did arrive, she was able to see Una sitting inside the window of the cafe. It was clear that Joan was in a very bad mood. Una offered to get her a coffee but she refused it. Joan then informed Una that she did not require her assistance anymore. She had been, by all appearances, discussing it with the other nurses and was so angry that she was not aware of the presence of other people in the cafe. Joan informed Una that nobody liked her and that Lorna Flannery, Pat Duggan and Bridget Quinn all disliked her and were saying how none of them wanted to work with her. Una however, was aware that although people in the cafe appeared to be occupied with their morning papers, nevertheless, they could not possibly avoid overhearing what was being said, which Una found very embarrassing and therefore did not retaliate in any way, but just agreed that it was fine. However, as the day wore on, Una began to worry about some of the things Joan had said to her earlier. When eventually she came in contact with Bridget Quinn, who was the most mature and refined of the nurses in Moss Town, Una asked her if there was any truth in what Joan had said earlier that day about all of them criticising her. Bridget agreed that there had been a lot of talk going on and suggested that Una's organiser be brought in on the discussions at this stage. Una agreed providing the nurses' organiser would also be present. At that point, Bridget rejected the idea.

The heavy lifting and the abuse Una had received over the years was beginning to take its toll and, to crown it all, she was feeling ill. When Una visited her doctor she was put off work for fourteen days. The first day of Una's sick leave, Pat Duggan phoned her, not to ask her how she was feeling, but to ask had she told Bridget Quinn what the other nurses had been saying about Bridget. Una told her that she had not and that she did not believe in stirring up trouble unless it was really necessary.

On the 3rd February 1986, the Help at Home organiser arranged a meeting for 3.00 p.m. for all of the full time Help at Homes. It was clear to Una right from the word go that she was in a foul mood. She accused all the helpers of being rude and bad mannered. Observing the situation, Una decided to say nothing. One of Una's colleagues did ask whether it was everyone in the group or was it just one or two, but was answered sternly by the organiser who asked her, "Would she fight with someone in the street? Would she go into a shop fighting with somebody?" The poor girl did not know what to say. Everybody else sat dumbfounded. It did however, leave Una wondering if the nurses had once more gone behind her back while she was on sick leave, reporting her and twisting things around. The organiser then turned her attention to Una saying the auditor had been and had queried her travel sheet. While Una was still on sick leave she received a letter from her organiser accompanied by a list of duties which Una was to cover when she returned to work. Covering Una's workload while she was sick were two full time Help at Home workers who were personal friends of Ann Hughes, the organiser. Everything seemed to point to the fact that either the nurses or the organiser's informants had told Ann Hughes about the disagreement between Una and Joan Moran.

Chapter 4

At that time, Una was a committee member of a Union. After the meeting on 3rd February, some of the staff who belonged to the same union as Una, complained to Una that if there was a complaint against someone then the individual involved should be told personally, in order that they could defend themselves against such complaints. Una offered to talk to the organiser about it but the girls advised her against it as she would only be abused. Knowing that something had to be done about it, Una told the assistant chairperson of the Union. When Ann Hughes received the complaint and asked her to meet with her in the organiser's office at 4 p.m. on 14th February, 1986, Una went to the office expecting the complaint might be about herself. Ann Hughes appeared very calm at first and asked Una several questions about her workload and also about the time she commenced work in the morning and the time she finished in the evening, which patient or client she called on first and in what rotation through the day and how much time she gave to each person. This she did not mind but such information could easily be found in her time sheet down to the last minute with each person. If Una was surprised about this, she was to be even more surprised when

Ann Hughes informed her that she could not, or would not, certify her travel sheet unless Una changed the figures on her travel sheet. Una could hardly believe her ears but remained cool and informed the organiser that she could not possibly do that. At this stage, the organiser got very angry and insisted that Una obey her. Una stood her ground and suggested that as she had her diary with her they should re-check it together and if there was a mistake in the travel sheet she would certainly alter it, but not otherwise. She would not let Una check her diary and furthermore she was only presenting a photostatic copy of Una's travel sheet, with Una's signature and the part where it should have been certified by the organiser as correct, excluded. The organiser was very angry at this stage and she seemed to have no control over her hands which were shaking. Una was aware that the situation was getting out of control and suggested taking the photostatic copy home with her, where she could check it against her diary and alter it if a mistake had been made. To this the organiser agreed.

It was a great hassle for Una to have to go through the whole month rechecking the travel sheet with her diary, only at the end to find there had been no mistake made in the first place. Una thought it best to write to her organiser and explain every detail of the mileage claimed.

Needless to say, this still did not satisfy her as Una received another letter from her organiser telling her to be in her office on 24th February, as Una's letter did not adequately answer her queries. At this stage, Una was really fed up with the harassment and the fact that she was convinced that her organiser was trying to frame her. It was by no means a pleasant experience being treated in this fashion and at the same time trying to meet the needs of the people she was visiting. It was only the support of her husband and other members of her family and the encouragement of the union she belonged to that helped her over this period.

On 28th February, Una received another letter from her organiser stating that their meeting on 24th February did not adequately answer her queries as regards Una's travel sheet and that she was passing the matter over to her immediate superior, who was Dr Moloney, director of the Blue Bell Board. Una was quite happy about this, as up to this stage at least, she had no bad experiences with doctors. Una's organiser was a nurse as there was a ruling in the Board that the Help at Home organiser had to be a nurse. It was not therefore surprising that she was on very friendly terms with the nurses in Moss Town. On 26th March, Una was asked to call to Dr Moloney's office. At that meeting also present was Chief Executive Officer, Andy Carmody. Andy was a member of the same union as Una and she had got to know him reasonably well through the union, but she was also aware of the fact that at this meeting he was wearing a different cap. Usually, Una would never agree to go to a meeting of this kind without being accompanied by a union representative but because she had got to know Andy Carmody, she had confidence in him and felt he would treat her in a fair manner. To say that Una was nervous would be an understatement as her organiser had threatened her on several occasions prior to this meeting as to what would happen to her at the meeting. At the meeting, the director outlined the organiser's report to Andy Carmody and Una and then explained how Una was replaced with two full time Help at Homes while she was on sick leave and that the organiser herself had also done Una's calls and all three had got the same mileage which was different to what Una had submitted. Mr Carmody kept reassuring Una that there was very little difference between her mileage and that of the other three. However, what the organiser had not said in her report was that the two Help at Homes were her personal friends and Una declined from saying so, as she was not of a catty nature. Dr Moloney questioned Una about the discrepancies in the mileage sheet. Una explained that the patients or clients had got used to her and trusted her and would ask her to deal with confidential matters which they would not ask a stranger to do. One of the queries was about an urgent prescription for a very ill man, something which should never have been queried in the first place. As a matter of fact, this man died in the local hospital a very short time later. Another query was about urgent shopping which would usually be delivered the following day but, because of the doctor's orders regarding her own health, Una was not going to be at work the following day.

The last charge against Una was the fact that her organiser had re-arranged her calls just before she returned from sick leave. Ann Hughes was so keen to find fault with Una's mileage that she overlooked the fact that she had re-arranged her calls. When Dr Moloney had listened to Una's explanation of the charges against her, she informed Una she was wiping the slate clean. She did, however, point out that because of the cutbacks Una was not allowed to visit patients or clients more than once a day. Regarding any errands they needed, Una must not return with them until her next visit, be that the next day or the next week. Una explained that she would be running the risk of having her car broken into and, what the patients or clients called their most valuable items, stolen if she were to use her car as a storage room. However, this was disregarded by both Dr Moloney and Andy Carmody as they both said that their cars were never yet broken into. Una agreed to the condition, but said she could not take responsibility for anything that went missing once she finished work in the evening.

Ann Hughes was also complaining that Una did not obey her. Una explained that she did obey her but she was aware that her organiser was trying to frame her. Andy Carmody suggested to Una that as Ann Hughes was her superior she should respect her. Una did not agree with this and explained that they did not get on very well together and that Ann Hughes had never earned Una's respect, as respect is something one has to earn and not demand. They were under the impression that Una was the only one having problems with the organiser, but she assured them that was not so, but that she was the only one to say anything about it. Una suggested that as she had two letters from her organiser accusing her of false mileage, she would like one clearing her of these charges. This was agreed to. Una was aware during the meeting that they both listened to her and she thanked them for doing so. Although Una came away from this meeting feeling happier than when she was going into it, she still felt a little sad as she could not help wondering how a little child in Ireland today could possibly make people, even those in senior positions, believe them when complaining of physical, mental or sexual abuse, when she as an adult with years of training and experience had such trouble getting anyone to believe her, or understand the strain and anxiety she underwent as a result of the harassment she had received.

Chapter 5

Although Una would visit the clinic with a message for the nurses when any of her patients or clients would request her to do so, or when she herself observed that they needed a nurse to visit them; she would also share a table with them in a cafe if it so happened that they were having their lunch break at the same time, she otherwise kept her distance as she no longer trusted them.

It was in April, 1986 that Una suspicions were aroused in earnest when she received her leave entitlement sheet and saw by it that her location of place of work was changed to Miltown instead of Moss Town as it had always been. The nurses had also being asking Una if she was she still working in Moss Town. When Una told them she was, they seemed surprised. However, when Una queried the change of location with her organiser she was told it was a mistake made in the main office and to change it back to Moss Town. Since Una did not approve of just altering documents of any kind without it being done officially, the heading remained Miltown, although Una's location remained Moss Town. Neither Una or Frances, the other Help at Home, although both based in Moss Town, hand any official place of record keeping or doing their monthly returns other than their cars or their private homes, which was very inconvenient. They also had no place from which to make official calls other than the public telephone booth. To make things more ridiculous, Una's starting point was the church as she entered Moss Town, while Frances' base was the corner shop on her entrance to Moss Town. The mistake that was made with the Help at Home service was it was started but never defined. It just drifted, each organiser making her own rules with the help of the nurses and the Help at Home workers having no say in the matter whatsoever.

It was by no means easy for Una to fit into this haphazard set up. She had become accustomed during her years in child care in England to joining in on discussions and making her views known and listening to other points of view. She was a strong believer in the fact that one should do their utmost to progress the service to which one belongs, not just for one's own sake but for the staff that came after them.

In the Blue Bell Board, the attitude was that if you do not like things as they are, then get out. Not Una's words, but Ann Hughes' word. The organiser still continued to query Una's travel sheet regarding mileage. At this stage she appeared to be in opposition to her supervisor, Dr Moloney and using Una to do so. She would call at a patient's house, when Una would be in the middle of her time allocated to that person, and inform Una that she wanted to see her at the local community centre which was usually their place of meeting. It would just turn out to be something trivial but it would mean that Una had to return to the patient she had been assisting. Una was aware that by obeying her organiser, she was disobeying Dr Moloney who had previously informed her that she must not return to the same person in one day.

This kind of harassment would drive the strongest personality insane. I often asked Una why she did not resign as I could see the traumatic affect it was having on her. Una's reply would always be the same, "That is just what she wants me to do." It was after one of these visits that Una's suspicions were aroused and she began to wonder if she was getting paid for the actual mileage she was submitting. On checking the money she received for her July 1986 mileage, she thought there was a discrepancy but did not do anything about it. When she received her August 1986 cheque, and again checked it, she again found a shortage in her money. At this stage she did query it and it was revealed by one of the finance officers that the mileage submitted to them by the Help at Home organiser did not correspond with the mileage submitted by Una. There was 17 miles withheld by the organiser. When Ann Hughes realised that Una had discovered the discrepancies she immediately contacted Una and asked if Una would agree to the 17 miles being added to her September 1986 mileage claim. For the first time ever, Una thought she looked concerned and Una, being soft hearted, agreed. When Una told the assistant chairman of her union he advised her to write to the executive officer asking for an explanation as to why it happened, which she did on 10th October 1986. The contents of the reply were to the effect that it was all to do with the cutbacks and that the organiser was acting on the authority vested in her position. When Una received this letter dated 14th October 1986, she was perplexed and very angry as it went against everything she believed to be right. Furthermore, it was leaving her without any rights whatsoever. Una again wrote to the executive officer on 16th October 1986 stating her concern and the fact that she would expect her organiser and any other person in a position of authority to have guidelines as to what they could do, and could not do, when interfering with the human rights of those beneath them.

As the executive officer had offered further assistance if necessary, Una also asked him if he would get her a photostatic copy of her August 1986 travel sheet as she was curious as to how the cuts were made. On 3rd November 1986 he again answered, informing Una that the letter was being passed to her organiser for attention. On the same date, the organiser wrote to Una saying she was surprised to hear that Una was looking for a copy of her August travel sheet as the money had already been passed for payment. Una did not bother to answer this letter. She told me she found it very upsetting to be treated in this manner and that all they were doing was passing the 'buck' from one to the other.

I was very much aware, and I know Una's family were also aware, of the terrible strain she was forced to undergo. Shortly after this, I noticed that Una appeared to be withdrawing from discussing anything with me. I would often try having a conversation with her as regards to what was happening at work but she would decline from discussing it. The confident, capable, challenging, yet trusting Una had vanished, and in her place a withdrawn, white faced person who appeared to be looking over her shoulder all the time and wondering what was going to happen to her next appeared. If she was less observant of what was going on around her, she may never have discovered the awful truth, or if the Blue Bell Board was more professional in their handling of the situation, she would never have suffered such pain and anxiety as a result of a minority of nurses making catty sneaky, unprofessional complaints in the first place.

Chapter 6

It was on one of her infrequent visits to the nurses' clinic in Moss Town, with a message for nurse Bridget Quinn from one of her patients, that Una became aware that there was an investigation going on. Pat Duggan, the nurse whom Una had helped the day after she crashed her car in November 1985, was the nurse that had reported Una in connection with her disagreement with nurse Joan Moran, the other nurse she had being helping at the time. At the inquiry, nurse Pat Duggan had been reprimanded and informed that she should not have reported Una unless it was something serious such as interfering with the welfare of one of her patients. In order to clear herself, Pat Duggan said that Una was interfering with her patients, and so keen was she to get herself off the hook, that she got a young, caring, visiting doctor in Moss Town into trouble, by saying that this doctor mistook Una as a nurse when he called on one of her patients, who was confined to a wheelchair. This patient complained of being constipated and the doctor gave him a suppository and left one with Una to give to the patient when required. Una was shocked when she discovered this, as on several occasions, when the nurses were friendly with Una, they would give her surgical gloves and microlax and ask if she would mind giving the patient she was visiting a microlax in order to save them a journey. They would also give Una dressings and ask her to replace a dressing for a patient until they got around to visiting that patient.

As it happened, this young doctor was cleared. Una had nursed her own mother during her terminal illness, and another doctor was able to verify that he had himself trained Una to use a drip and give suppositories and other forms of caring to keep her mum at home. At this stage, Una's health was failing and on many of her visits to her own doctor, he tried without success to discover if Una was aware of what was going on. Unfortunately, he could not tell her in case she did not know. Una had got to the stage that she really did not know whom she could trust. Any person who has been repeatedly harassed knows this feeling all too well.

On 26th May 1987, there was a meeting of all the full time Help at Home staff. There were about 16 of them spread out over different areas in the community, and they would usually only get together at a meeting such as this, which was arranged only occasionally. At this meeting the organiser informed all of them that the auditor was now visiting her office and requested their 1986 diaries. Una, being aware of all the evidence her 1986 diary contained, decided on the spur of the moment that there was no way the organiser was going to get possession of her diary, as she might just be planning to confiscate the evidence. Una informed her that she would not send in her diary but that she would take it in and sit down with the auditor and answer any questions he may have regarding her mileage. The organiser made a note of this and said she would tell the auditor.

At this stage, Una was having a lot of pain in her stomach and chest, at intervals. Her doctor sent her for tests at the local hospital. The result of each test was the same; they could not find anything wrong with her. This worried Una in case people would think that she was imagining it. It was during one of her visits to her doctor, after getting the results of one of these tests that Una confided in him about the pressure she was undergoing and the reason for it and of her growing fear that nobody would believe her regarding the pain she was suffering. Her doctor was an understanding gentleman who reassured Una that he believed her, and that he would make arrangements for her to go into a hospital of her choice as soon as she was ready to do so.

Chapter 7

At this stage, the cutbacks were really being put into practice. There were no relief staff to replace the nurses when they were off duty. The same applied to the Help at Homes. Una was very much aware that the nurses were concerned in case some of them would be made redundant and the Help at Homes used to carry out some of their duties such as washing and changing patients. The nurses would try to trick Una into using the word 'bed bath' which was pathetic and just playing with words. This was an expression Una never used and would refer to that part of her caring as washing and changing the patient, be they bed bound or mobile.

On 22nd June 1987, Una again visited her doctor and, realising that she could not endure any more pressure, he put her on sick leave. On 23rd June 1987, Una received a letter from her organiser requesting her to send in her 1986 diary with her monthly returns. Una had already explained to her on 26th May 1987 that she would take in her diary to the auditor when requested by him to do so, and as she was at present on sick leave, she ignored the organiser's letter. She did however phone the auditor at the Blue Bell Board who informed Una that he did not require her diary but suggested that it may be an auditor from an independent body. He told Una he would make enquiries with the staff in his department about it and phone her back. He however, never did phone back.

On 1st July 1987, Una was admitted to a private hospital and although a little nervous at first was soon made to feel at ease by the staff there. Undergoing tests at this hospital, it was discovered that Una was suffering from a hiatus hernia and an ulcer as a result of the hernia, which was causing the severe pain she was complaining of. Una told me afterwards that at times the pain was so severe that she thought she was going to die. It was a great relief to discover what her ailment was and to be receiving treatment for it.

When Una was discharged from hospital she visited her doctor and complimented him on his diagnosis as he kept reassuring Una before she was admitted to hospital that he thought it was an ulcer despite the negative x-rays at the local hospital. The medication prescribed for Una helped her a great deal but also made her feel very tired and as a result had to spend a lot of time in bed. Una was more open with her doctor at this stage and was able to discuss things with him more freely. Earlier, she had found it difficult to be open with him about the harassment and she felt embarrassed discussing with him what the nurses had done to her. She felt let down as she was under the impression that the nurses were her friends and also felt that one must not criticise the nurses with the medical profession or vice versa.

When I visited Una, she appeared much more relaxed and told me it was great to be away from all the harassment and to be able to do just as she liked. I was aware however that deep down she was feeling very angry about the whole episode.

On 5th November 1987, Una received a registered letter from Dr Lynne Daly, Acting Director of the Blue Bell Board, requesting that Una return her 1986 diary immediately as an auditor by the name of Gerard Stevens was demanding it. This was again something that should never have happened if the Help at Home organiser had informed the auditor that Una wished to take in her diary and answer any queries regarding her routes or her mileage. Instead, the organiser told the auditor that Una had refused to send in her diary. In turn, the auditor decided to obtain the diary under court order. Being aware of the anger and resentment which Una had bottled up for so long, I was not surprised when I learned that she had written to the acting Director informing her that she was still on sick leave and that the harassment she received while working for the Blue Bell Board was the major cause of her illness. Una also stated that the diary was her only record and evidence of the harassment she had received. She did however, explain that she did not in any way want to prevent the auditor from carrying out his duties and therefore, she would allow him to visit her home where he could check her diary and she would answer any of his queries. When the union realised what was happening, and what the consequences could be, they advised Una to phone the auditor herself and make arrangements to take in her diary which she did. I discovered later that the auditor learned that the organiser was trying to use him to put pressure on Una. Una told me afterwards that she was very nervous on her way to discuss the contents of her diary with the auditor in case he would find something wrong. Because she was still on a lot of tablets she felt nervous about driving there and, on the whole, felt very vulnerable.

The sad thing about any responsible body allowing an individual to be treated as Una was over the years is that it is not just the individual who suffers but the immediate family also and they can be made to feel very inadequate as how best to deal with the problem. The auditor stressed the point to Una that he could obtain the diary through the court. He also informed Una that she could sue the Blue Bell Board for the way she had been treated.

Only somebody who has experienced harassment will be fully aware of the extent of damage which can be caused by such abuse. Una's confidence and self-esteem could have be completely destroyed. Therefore it is of the utmost importance that if there is the slightest inkling that if an employee is being harassed it should be investigated immediately by the employer and dealt with in a professional manner in order to prevent unnecessary suffering to the employee. Any well organised firm should be capable of doing this. I can only emphasise once more how uncaring and unprofessionally the Blue Bell Board behaved by ignoring the fact that Una was being harassed over a period of many the years and by sweeping it under the carpet every time it was brought to light.

Now, the 23rd June 1988, one year later, Una is still on sick leave and as yet cannot talk about her organiser or the nurses in Moss Town without getting upset. One of the reasons I decided to write this book was to use it as a means of therapy by getting Una to talk about her experiences and to reassure her that I cared enough to want to do something about it. Una's own words were, "If it only helps to prevent somebody else being harassed and having to endure it as I did, some good will come of it." I do know that Una will never again be as trusting as she was before all this happened. I can only hope and pray that the old saying, "time heals all wounds", will one day come true for Una.

Chapter 8

In order that the following pages of this book are understood and appreciated, it is necessary to write a little about the unprofessional behaviour of a minority of nurses, and the cruel and nasty way in which Una's mum and family, including Una herself, were treated. All of which led to the family's decision to keep their mother at home and have her on a drip there for the last few months of her life with the help and guidance of the local general practitioner.

The hospital in question was a very busy hospital which catered for most of the patients surrounding the Blue Bell Board, and because of this there was often a long wait before the patient would be allocated a bed in a ward. They would be left for hours on a stretcher-like bed in casualty or sitting in a waiting room. This was to say, at the least, very frustrating for both patient and relations. However, it would not have been too bad if one could be sure that their elderly relations would be treated with kindness and respect after being sent to the ward. The times Una's mum was in this hospital was always stressful. It was very clear to Una that there was something very wrong with the supervision of the ward where her mum was being treated, and although everybody was pleasant enough to Una and other members of the family at first, there was a lot of hassle going on with relatives of other patients, and it was misinterpreted to the extent that it gave one the impression that it was the relatives that were causing the trouble. However, Una, her mum and other members of the family were soon to experience first-hand what other families had previously been through. Things finally came to a head when Una's mum was admitted to the hospital because she was very ill and dehydrated and needed to be put on a drip. The family were all very concerned about her, and the fact that she hated the idea of going into that hospital made it worse. One evening, when Una was visiting her mum, one of the nurses informed her that she was going to leave a bed pan on the chair by her mother's bed that night and that her mother would have to use it herself instead of calling the nurses. Una was very concerned about this and asked the nurse how on earth she expected an 81 year old lady, on a drip, to be able to use a bed pan by herself. The nurse replied that no way would she be running to her with a bed pan for her to use during the night adding that none of her other nursing colleagues would do so either. That was the last time the family ever allowed their mum to be admitted to hospital, but before she was discharged on that occasion she endured terrible abuse and ill treatment. Her relatives' hands were tied even though they did complain. The hospital closed ranks. It was only the fact that Una was employed by the Blue Bell Board that prevented her from publicising it at the time.

It was very difficult for the family caring for their mum at home. Her bedroom was like a private room in a hospital, but the local G.P. was an outstanding doctor, and although it must have been a big strain on him, he did everything possible to make the last few months of her life as comfortable as possible.

I am pleased to be able to say that the casualty department at the hospital where Una's mum had been ill-treated were also very helpful .They supplied the drips and the sister was also very kind to Una when she called to collect them. If Una had been treated in a fair way when she returned to work a few weeks after the death of her mum, I am sure she would have been happy to forget the whole episode, and just get on with her life but the previous pages of this book emphasise how very badly she was treated. In fact, she should never have returned to work. Strangely enough, it was a while before Una connected the treatment she was receiving and her sticking up for her mum as one and the same. I worried about her going back to work because she did not seem to expect anything like that to happen, however when it did dawn on her why all this was happening, it was years before she would allow anyone to send her to that hospital. She looked on it as an unsafe place. It is only in very recent years that she has allowed any doctor to send her there, however, her husband and father and brothers did use it. But, I understood how she felt and her husband supported her decision. It was a long time before the Blue Bell Board became aware of the fact that Una was not using their hospitals and they did not like it. I mentioned earlier that Una was admitted to a private hospital where it was discovered that she had an ulcer which was causing her severe pain. Her husband liked that hospital and he often used it himself without any hassle. When the Blue Bell Board realised how Una was feeling about their hospitals, they should have done everything in their power to convince Una that they would make sure she would be safe, but they did a very unprofessional thing, they branded her as being mental and talked about her in these terms on the on local radio and in the daily newspapers. They basically blacklisted her so that she could not be treated in their hospitals, thereby covering themselves. Una told me that a nurse told her it just went to show how closely knit the profession is. Una asked me, "Do tinkers not behave in the same way? Do they not fight between themselves and then gang together when they feel threatened?" She said it is classed as unsociable behaviour when tinkers did it, but professional behaviour when members of the nursing profession did it. The title of this book, 'Who Dares to Tread' relates to the extraordinary difficulties Una faced when trying to stick up for the rights of her relatives because of the way they were being neglected and, in some instances, ill-treated by the medical establishment.

Chapter 9

When Una went on sick leave on June 22nd 1989, nobody, including Una, anticipated that she would be off work for almost two years, and I should imagine that the Blue Bell Board were playing with time. At the end of two years she would cease to exist as an employee. Then a strange thing happened, two of Una's colleagues phoned Una to tell her that they were being harassed by the organiser and that the organiser was being supported by another colleague who was a personal friend. Una was feeling sorry for them both, because she had a good idea how they must be feeling. This gave Una a little boost also as she no longer felt alone. The three of them arranged to meet, and when they went to meet the union representative, Una also went with them. However, by this time Una's two colleagues had resigned as they could not stand the harassment. The union took both cases to the Labour Court and lost one case, but won the other. As far as Una's case was concerned, the union representative was saying Una did not have a case because her job was there for her. The representatives did however, agree to meet officials of the Blue Bell Board with her and thrash out her case. Una was now meeting with the union on her own. The then chairman of the union made

Una tell him over and over again about the harassment. Una would always tell him the same story, but it was very stressful for her and she would always cry after talking about it. The union was now putting pressure on the Blue Bell Board about the way Una had been treated. However, the union told Una that they would not be taking the case to a tribunal even though Una thought she had a good case and that it should be tried in court.

Shortly after this, the Blue Bell Board put more pressure on Una and used a consultant physician to do so. On January 17th 1989, Una received a letter asking her to attend for a private medical at the residence of a consultant physician. The appointment was made for January 26th at 3.00 p.m. Una went along as requested. This consultant also practiced at the hospital where Una's mum had previously been ill-treated, but was not aware of what had taken place at that time. The Blue Bell Board had presented all the dates of Una's absence on sick leave to the consultant and the first dates that he asked Una about were June 30th 1981 - September 4th 1981. Una explained that she had flu and bronchitis, and that her illness was prolonged by an emotional upset. The doctor asked her if she would like to tell him about it and what had upset her. Una told him that her mum had been ill-treated whilst in the local hospital. The doctor immediately told Una that she was imagining all that and that it was not true. This upset Una and she panicked as this was a repeat of her previous experiences of not being believed. By right, that doctor should have cancelled the medical until he furnished himself with the correct information but the system was such that the doctor had to send in a medical report. Una's husband drove her for her medical that day and he told me afterwards that when Una came out she looked pale and upset and a lot worse than before she went in.

On another occasion, sometime later, when Una was made go for another medical with the same doctor, he informed Una that he had since made enquiries and had found that the facts which she told him previously were indeed true. On June 16th 1989, Una returned to work, but not before officials of the Blue Bell Board agreed to meet Una and union representatives. That meeting took place on March 8th 1989. Una's medical report went against her, and although she contested it, everyone thought she should return to work for a little while at least and see how things would work out.

It could be said that Una's return to work was doomed right from the word go. On June 13th 1989, Una received a letter from the staff officer of the Board stating that he was in receipt of her medical certificate and, as she was fit to resume work as a full time help at home, to report to the Help At Home organiser at 9.30 a.m. on June 16th. On the same date, Una received a letter from her organiser saying to arrange to meet her in her office at 9.30 a.m. on June 16th. On the morning in question, Una went to the organiser's office as requested. Una was there first, and when the organiser arrived, she greeted Una in a cool, distant manner. Una was given several official forms to sign. Her organiser then informed her that she would be based in Miltown. You may remember that I mentioned earlier in this book how on one occasion when Una's leave sheet was marked Miltown that her organiser told her to change it, that it was a mistake. So, on this occasion, Una told her organiser that she did not receive a letter telling her that her base was being changed. With that, the organiser got up from her chair and said to Una, "Well you can now tell that to the director, she is waiting in her office to see you." Dr Moloney and Michael Stevenson, the new Chief Executive Officer, were in the office when Una arrived. Andy Carmody who had been the executive officer the last time Una had been in that office, had taken early retirement while Una was on sick leave.

Dr Moloney and Michael Stevenson shook hands with Una and welcomed her back. Her organiser had followed Una to the director's office and Una immediately felt at a disadvantage. But, Una did query her base being changed. Michael Stevenson explained to Una that the Board can do that, and Una sensed that he had himself been moved against his wishes, so Una agreed to give it a try. If there were none of the nurses from Moss Town visiting any of the patients or clients that Una was visiting, it may have made some sense. However, Pat Duggan, the nurse who had previously told the Help at Home organiser to put pressure on Una was herself visiting at least one of the same families. Una was hoping that she would not make any more trouble for her. Una classed her as being very dangerous. Earlier, when it was being investigated as to whether Una had interfered with the rights of one of Pat Duggan's patients, Una had overheard Pat telling the other nurses that if Una's doctor told Una about the investigation, then she would no longer have him as her doctor. For reasons of his own he did not tell Una, but I don't think it was because he was frightened of losing Pat as a patient.

Chapter 10

Una would have preferred it if she had been allowed to work closer to her own home, and not have to do so much driving. However, she soon got used to working in Miltown and looked forward to receiving her pay each week. When she worked at Moss Town her pay was mailed to her each week, now that she was based in Miltown, she had to collect it from her organiser's office each Friday. If, for some reason, Una was not working on the Friday, she would not get paid until she returned to work as the office was sixteen miles from her home. The organiser continued to harass Una every chance she got. Most of it would be subtle harassment. For instance, when Una would go to her office to collect her pay her organiser would sit lecturing her while at the same time waving her pay in front of her. Una told me that one of these days she would just grab it and tell her that the pay belonged to her, but she never did.

Having to go into the office where she had previously been so badly harassed was not easy for Una and she would have to go to the toilet several times before going in. I remember on more than one occasion, Una telling me that her organiser travelled some distance to ask her to report to her office just to get her to sign a form. Una told me that she had written to head office asking for her pay to be mailed to her home as she was finding it stressful having to go into the organiser's office and ask for it, but still nothing was done about it. Sending Una back to work under the same person, and letting her be continuously harassed was ludicrous, and it was not long before Una was back on sick leave because she was vomiting blood and although she did return to work it was not for long. Her organiser was continuously accusing her of being cheeky and rude and finding fault with her work and she arranged her work load to the extent that Una lost confidence in herself and gave up the ghost and decided that rather than resign she would try and get early retirement.

On the 30th March 1990, Una submitted a letter seeking early retirement on health grounds. It was accompanied by a letter from her doctor who had been very supportive to her all the way. By this time, Una did not want any communication whatsoever with the Help at Home organiser, so she sent her letter to the Executive Officer, Michael Stevenson, and in it she stated that the Blue Bell Board were aware of the circumstances which had been a major contributory factor to her present health conditions. Tests carried out later proved this correct. On April 24th, Una received a letter from the personnel officer requesting her to attend for a private medical on the same date at 3.00 p.m. but Una refused as she did not get sufficient notice. The next appointment was made for Tuesday 8th May 1990, which Una attended. On that occasion, the doctor certified Una as unfit to return to work and from that date Una ceased to be an employee of the Blue Bell Board. She had qualified for early retirement on health grounds. Since then Una has improved and is looking much better.

Early in August 1990, Una was sent by her doctor for a mammogram at one of the Blue Bell Board hospitals. Una was not aware at the time that the hospital of her choice did not have that type of X-ray. So, when the doctor suggested admitting her, Una asked if she could go to the private hospital because she felt safe there. Most of the doctors in the Blue Bell hospitals also had beds in the private hospital, but management would not allow Una to have the X-ray in the Blue Bell Board hospital and be admitted to the private hospital. So it was mid-December before Una was admitted to a hospital in Dublin, 174 miles from her own home. By this time, 'the powers that be' were very angry about Una not using the Blue Bell hospitals and decided to try and prove that Una needed psychiatric help. Una was aware that she was being assessed and it made her feel very uncomfortable. Under the very badly conceived Irish Mental Health Act, if Una's husband was not aware of the harassment Una received and if he could be persuaded that Una was imagining everything, he could be asked to sign for Una to be admitted to a psychiatric hospital. However, Una's husband knew very well that she was not imagining things. He also knew that Una was very strong willed and would not allow herself to be admitted to a hospital where she did not feel safe and he supported her. One could say that he himself had suffered through the experiences which Una had gone through.

Although Una would not allow herself to be admitted to any of the Blue Bell Board hospitals, she would not in any way interfere with the rights of another person to be admitted, providing she knew that they themselves would be happy about it and she proved this to be correct when an uncle who lived with herself and her husband got a severe stroke on 28th January 1991. Neither would she allow her own feelings to prevent her from visiting the hospital. But Una assessed that the hospital staff may not have coped quite as well having Una visit and watch what was going on during the day. For the first five days or so her uncle was in a public ward. Then he was transferred to a private ward. This was justified by saying that he had diarrhoea and they were protecting the other patients. He had been on an intravenous drip and they had started feeding him through a tube in his nose and it was therefore understandable that this may cause the upset. So, Una assumed that he was being put into a private ward just to save their own blushes. As it happened, it was good for him to be in a private ward as it was as near as possible to being at home and he improved for a little while. When the private ward was required for a private patient, Una's uncle was transferred back to the public ward. Some of the nurses, who were aware of the fact that Una did not use the hospital for herself and were feeling angry about it, were saying within earshot of her that what was good for the goose should be good for the gander. Una pretended not to hear them, but that kind of behaviour does not improve matters, it only makes things worse.

Chapter 11

I have tried to emphasise throughout this book that I am only writing about Una's experiences while working for the Blue Bell Board and although I had, at times, to touch on incidents which were not directly connected with her work, I did that in order to give an insight of what was occurring in her life previously and immediately afterwards. I cannot stress strongly enough that Una is by no means judging all nurses by her bad experiences. The nurses who behaved unprofessionally were in a minority and in reasonably senior positions, probably not because they were most suitably qualified for the positions they held, but often because they had pull at the top.

However, it was wrong for management to allow anybody to be treated in that manner and it has to be condemned at the highest possible level. The fact that they then refused to allow X-rays to be carried out and released in order that Una could continue to use a hospital where she always felt safe must also be condemned.

On December 7th a friend of Una's collected a letter from her doctor's receptionist. Una was being admitted to a private hospital in Dublin two days later. On December 9th, Una was up early as she was catching the 7.39 a.m. train from Mosstown to Dublin. Una's husband drove her to the station and although during the previous day it had been snowing heavily, the 12 mile road they had to travel was not too bad and they got to the station in plenty of time for Una to catch the train. Her husband wanted to go with her but Una wanted to go alone. She felt that by doing so she was proving to society that she was not 'nutty' as she was aware of most of the things that were being said about her. She was also aware of the bad feelings about her not using the Blue Bell Board hospitals. Who could blame her after her past experiences?

Now, she was quite excited about going to a hospital in Dublin. She was not sure what the X-rays would show up, but for the time being at least she felt she had won, and for someone who was harassed as severely as Una had been, winning was very important. It was not just for the sake of winning, but for the sake of justice. When Una arrived in Dublin she had something to eat at a nearby hotel, then she hired a taxi to take her to the hospital. As she had never been in that particular hospital before she did not know what to expect. However, Una was soon made to feel welcome, but as she was not supposed to be allowed to talk to anybody other than the hospital staff, she was put into a private room on admission. After being examined by the house doctor, Una told her that she would prefer to be in a ward with other patients rather than a private ward. The doctor told Una that she would see the matron and Una was moved into a four bedded ward where she was very happy. Later that day, Una meet the medical physician and remembered that she had met him briefly about six months earlier. Una liked him then and thought she was happy that it was him that had her admitted. It was great after such a long wait to be having all the necessary tests carried out and to be given the results so promptly.

The Hospital in question did not have the X-ray equipment to carry out all the tests he required, but when that was the case he would make arrangements to have the tests carried out in another private hospital where he had his offices. In the hospital where Una was admitted she was very much aware that she was admitted as a mentally ill patient, as that is how the so-called experts in the Blue Bell Board had branded her, all because she would not stand by and watch her mother being ill-treated and abused. To brand her mentally ill was their way of covering up. Una knows now that she should never have returned to work for them after her mother's death.

A psychiatrically trained nurse was sent with Una when she went to the other hospital to have a mammogram but Una did not mind. They talked a lot and found they had a lot in common. At one stage, when Una was advising her about a problem in the nurse's own family, she laughed and said, "So you're the one the Board is calling mental. There must be something very wrong there."

When Una went to the same hospital for a MRI scan, she was allowed to go alone. Una was aware that there was a bit of aggravation going on at times about the tests that her Doctor had her booked for at the hospital where she was admitted for a colonoscopy. Una's doctor was determined that he was having this test done even if he had to take her to the hospital where he had his clinic.

The staff there were saying that they had the theatre booked to start at 8 a.m. and could not fit Una's test in, so a team came in from another hospital, but they had to be out of the theatre by 8a.m., which they were. The nurses would only do what they really had to do for Una. They were backing their colleagues, after all, most of them came from the same area, but Una did not let their behaviour get to her. The domestic supervisor put on a show one day and her staff were with her. The patients were saying to Una that she was very strict with the staff, but Una told them to take no notice that it was just a stage show. Una used that hospital several times after that and found that everyone treated her well. Una was very lucky that she had nice patients sharing her ward and they often had a good laugh. Una was no longer working and she was now on medication to improve her physical health by the doctor who was treating her in Dublin. Una's husband was now having health worries. Una wanted him to go and see the doctor who was treating her in Dublin but he had a lot of trust in his own doctor and although Una told him that she believed that he too was blacklisted by the Blue Bell Board, he still thought his doctor would look after him. One day, when he was very ill, his doctor sent him to the local hospital by ambulance, but on arrival at the hospital he was indeed refused treatment by the nurses. The Garda were called because his life was in danger and as it was a public hospital they had no right to refuse him treatment. In the end a young doctor on duty took care of him. Her husband actually had a cardiac arrest whilst the doctor was working on him and had to be rushed to the intensive care unit. He was in the unit for about three weeks but he was very well treated whilst he was there. When he was due to come out on the ward, he wanted a private room but there was not a vacant one. He did not like the ward he was put into and every time the doctor came to do anything with him, Una had to get out. In fact, she was told to go which did not help. He was discharged the day after he came out of the intensive care, and two weeks later he died at home on their living room floor waiting for the ambulance to arrive. Una and his G.P. were with him but there was nothing the doctor could do. He needed to be in hospital. Una thought about suing the hospital and the Blue Bell Board for neglect but she thought that her two brothers, who lived nearby, would also be neglected. That is the way the system works. When the last of Una's two brothers died, she then took the case to the European Court of Human Rights. Nurses who worked in the hospital where Ulna and her husband were blacklisted, told Ulna that they could help her because they were on holiday if she needed help, but that they would not be allowed to help her if they were at work.

Una asked me, "What you think of that? What kind of country are we living in for that to be allowed in the first place?"

The Court of Human Rights said she did not give them any proof that she was blacklisted. Of course, if she had given the nurses names, they would have lost their jobs, so she lost the case. The ill treatment of her mum and the harassment was out of date. The Court found that her case should have been taken into the High Court when it was happening. Una had talked to the family solicitor about it when she became aware of what was going on but that solicitor was working for the Blue Bell Board at the time and could not take a case against them and, although he did offer to give her the name of a Solicitor who could help her, Una left feeling bewildered about it all. It's only very recently that Una has allowed any doctor to send her to the local

Blue Bell Board hospital. When she does go there, and a doctor decides that she needs a scan done if her blood tests shows that she is bleeding and they need to find out from where, Una is not told anything about it until she asks a doctor hours later if they have forgotten about her. By then it is too late to go for the scan so she usually ends up having to go to another hospital in order to get tests done that could be done at the local hospital. But, one would never be able to prove that. That is being blacklisted. It is so cunning and a game to them. One may ask, "Will she ever again feel safe in their local hospitals?" I think the answer is probably, No!

No one has ever even apologised to Una, which is very sad, but the possibility of any form of medical board or medical staff blacklisting a patient on the basis of lies and innuendo is an appalling situation and everything possible both organisationally and at the level of human resources management should be done to make sure this sort of thing can never happen again.

The End

Made in the USA
Charleston, SC
02 April 2014